FOREWORD

I'll be honest with you. We are small.
CRAZY small.

Crazy Lazy Thanksgiving Gravy small.

To put it in perspective, if the entire Milky Way
Galaxy was the size of a grain of sand, the entire
universe would be as big as the Empire State Building.

Nuts, right*?!?!?*

Some of the stuff in this book is so BIG that our brains can't even
comprehend it, but hang in there. I promise we'll have some fun.

—Mr. DeMaio

DEDICATION

"We are the middle children of history. Born too late to explore
earth, born too early to explore space."

—Anonymous

This book is for my space nuts out there.

While this quote may be true to some, it doesn't have to be.
Yes, it's too late for me, but it isn't too late for you!

If you are interested in the far reaches of the universe, do
something about it and prove that anonymous person wrong.
I dare you!

—Mr. DeMaio

MR. DeMAIO
PRESENTS!

THE BIGGEST STUFF
IN THE UNIVERSE

by **Mr. DeMaio**

illustrated by **Saxton Moore**

GROSSET & DUNLAP

TABLE OF CONTENTS

BIGGEST
EAR
WHY DO THEY MOCK ME?!? WHY?!?!?
WHAT'S HIS PROBLEM?
PROBABLY AN EARACHE . . .

THE BIGGEST STUFF ON EARTH

THE WORLD'S BIGGEST GUMMY BEAR

The largest gummy bear sold today weighs twenty-six pounds. That's as heavy as three eight-pound bowling balls!

THIS GUMMY BEAR IS 17 INCHES TALL!

GUYS! I THINK I CAN SEE THROUGH ALL SPACE AND TIME.

It has 32,000 calories. That's more than most people eat in twelve days!

And it has 5,035 grams of sugar! That's as much as 315 doughnuts!

I WONDER WHO THE FIRST GUY WAS THAT LOOKED AT A REAL BEAR AND SAID, "LET'S MAKE THAT EXACT SAME THING, BUT MADE OF CANDY."

YOU THINK THAT'S GROSS? IMAGINE THE GUY WHO INVENTED THE GUMMY WORM!

THE BIGGEST ANIMAL . . . EVER!

THE BLUE WHALE

Some blue whales can grow to be up to 100 feet long. That's longer than two school buses!

100 FEET!

And some are believed to weigh up to 330,000 pounds! That's as heavy as twenty-three adult elephants.

x23

THE BIGGEST ANIMAL . . . EVER! (cont'd)

THE BLUE WHALE

About 100 adults could fit inside a blue whale's mouth.

A blue whale's tongue weighs as much as about two adult hippos.

JEEZ. WHAT A WEIRD LOOKIN' HORSE. I SHALL NAME YOU . . . CHUNKENSTEIN.

THE LARGEST TREE ON EARTH ... and Everywhere Else (probably)

GENERAL SHERMAN

General Sherman is nearly 275 feet high! That's almost the length of three blue whales.

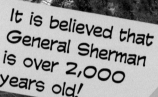

It is believed that General Sherman is over 2,000 years old!

The tree is about 52,500 cubic feet in volume. That's equal to nearly half the volume of an Olympic-size swimming pool.

YOU GUYS LIED! THERE'S NO ARCADE UP HERE!!! OH! A BLUE JAY!

Some branches on General Sherman have a diameter of almost seven feet! That's bigger than Major League Baseball player Aaron Judge!

If you were to measure General Sherman around its base, it would be about 102 feet in circumference!

THE BIGGEST LIVING THING ON EARTH
ARMILLARIA OSTOYAE

The fungus is estimated to be anywhere from 2,400 to 8,650 years old!

The blue whale is big, but not even close to as huge as this fungus in eastern Oregon. This fungus takes up an area as big as almost 1,700 football fields!

almost x1,700

This humongous fungus is believed to weigh over 35,000 tons! That's more than 160 times heavier than a blue whale!

x160

The large clumps of yellowish-brown mushrooms that appear above the ground are the fruiting parts of a much bigger organism that lies within the ground, out of sight, making it pretty much invisible from the surface.

MUSHROOMS . . . WHY'D IT HAVE TO BE MUSHROOMS?

WEIRD ALIEN WITH GLASSES. WHY'D IT HAVE TO BE A WEIRD ALIEN WITH GLASSES?

THE HUGEST-est-EST BUILDING EVER MADE

BURJ KHALIFA

The Burj Khalifa's tip reaches 2,700 feet. That's as much as twenty-seven blue whales or three Eiffel Towers!

The Burj Khalifa also has the highest restaurant in the world. It serves food 1,447 feet in the air!

I WISH EVERYTHING WAS MEASURED IN BLUE WHALES!

HOW LONG DO YOU HAVE TO BE TO RIDE THIS ROLLER COASTER? HALF A BLUE WHALE!

It was built using nearly nine million pounds of steel!

If you were to line up all the steel used in a row, it would span a quarter of the way around the Earth.

The Burj Khalifa has nearly 3,000 stairs!

THE (Kinda) BIGGEST MOUNTAIN ON EARTH
MOUNT EVEREST

Mount Everest is over 29,000 feet high. That's more than ten Burj Khalifas!

Scientists estimate that Mount Everest grows about two inches each year. That's almost as much as a young boy grows in a year.

×10

WHENEVER I TRY TO LISTEN TO MY HEARTBEAT, I HEAR KID ROCK SONGS FROM 1998. IS THAT NORMAL?

. . . YES.

At Everest's highest point, due to the atmospheric pressure, you breathe in a third of the amount of oxygen you would normally breathe.

HEY, GUYS! AM I HALLUCINATING OR DID JUSTIN GET THE NUMBER TWENTY-FIVE TATTOOED ON HIS FACE?

THE (Kinda) BIGGEST MOUNTAIN ON EARTH
MOUNT EVEREST (cont'd)

Sir Edmund Hillary and Sherpa Tenzing Norgay were the first to successfully get to the summit of Mount Everest in 1953. Tenzing Norgay unsuccessfully tried to get to the top of Everest six times before reaching it with his friend Sir Edmund.

It takes roughly two months to climb to the top! That's as long as your summer vacation!

BOW BEFORE ME, EARTHLINGS. FOR I AM YOUR RULER!

Mount Everest is the highest mountain above sea level, but there's an even bigger mountain that stretches beneath the ocean. Mauna Kea in Hawaii is about 3,000 feet higher than Everest when you measure it from its base, which is 19,700 feet below the water's surface.

SPPIII-SPPPPIII-SSSSPIIII . . .

One living thing has been found near the top: the Himalayan jumping spider. This spider has been seen on the mountain at heights up to 22,000 feet!

NOW LEAVING EARTH!
Home of the Man with the World's Largest Ear
WHY WORLD?!?!?
WHY?!?!?!?

THE BIGGEST STUFF IN SPACE!

- Mega-Size Space Volcano
- Largest Asteroid
- Gigantor Superstorm
- Most Biggest Planet in Our Solar System

THE MEGA-SIZE SPACE VOLCANO

OLYMPUS MONS

Olympus Mons is believed to be about 72,000 feet high! That's almost three times the size of Mount Everest and as big as twenty-six Burj Khalifas!

MOUNT EVEREST x 3? I MUST HAVE BEEN ABSENT THAT DAY IN SCHOOL.

EHHH . . . I'M MORE OF A SWORD VOLCANO KINDA GUY.

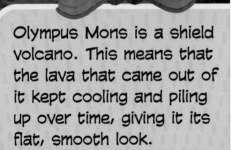

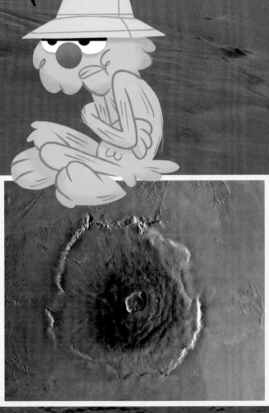

Olympus Mons is a shield volcano. This means that the lava that came out of it kept cooling and piling up over time, giving it its flat, smooth look.

THE MEGA-SIZE SPACE VOLCANO
OLYMPUS MONS (cont'd)

Some volcanoes on Mars are up to 100 times bigger than the ones on Earth!

Olympus Mons could cover the entire state of Arizona.

THESE COULD BE OUR LAST MOMENTS TOGETHER, GUYS!!!

There are three other giant shield volcanoes right near Olympus Mons. Their names are Ascraeus Mons, Pavonis Mons, and Arsia Mons.

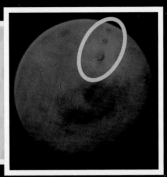

It is believed that because Olympus Mons is so high, if you were able to stand at its summit, you could see the curvature of Mars!

I CAN'T DIE NOW! I HAVE SO MANY QUESTIONS!!!

LIKE WHAT?

IS THERE ANY RICE IN RICE KRISPIES? DOES CHOCOLATE MILK COME FROM BROWN COWS? DO TURTLES THINK FROGS ARE HOMELESS?!!!

WELCOME TO . . . FIND . . . THE HIDDEN . . . PICTURES!

TRY TO FIND . . .

- A red rock
- A kinda darker red rock
- Some red dirt
- Seventy-two more red rocks

THE LARGEST ASTEROID
(Sort of)
4 VESTA

CERES! SET MY ALARM FOR 3:00 P.M.!

Ceres was called the largest asteroid for many years, but it is so much bigger than its rocky neighbors in the asteroid belt between Mars and Jupiter that scientists classified it as a dwarf planet in 2006.

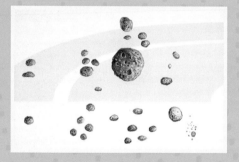

4 Vesta is believed to be about 329 miles wide. That's fifteen times bigger than the width of the English Channel!

ENGLAND

×15

FRANCE

4 Vesta is one of the brightest rocky bodies ever observed in our solar system. The bright material is believed to come from its native rocks.

I LIKE HOW SHE'S JUST CASUALLY HOLDING A SNAKE . . . AND A PLATE.

EHHHH! I'M MORE OF A VESTA 3 KINDA GUY. THE BEST PART IS WHEN HE'S SLOWLY LOWERED INTO THE LAVA BUT GIVES A THUMBS-UP BEFORE HE DIES!

VESTA

VESTAE   SACRVM
C. PVPIVS FIRMINVS ET
MVDASENA   TROPHIME

4 Vesta is named after the goddess of the hearth and household in Roman mythology.

THE GIGANTOR SUPERSTORM
THE GREAT RED SPOT

The Great Red Spot on Jupiter stretches over 10,000 miles wide! Two to three Earth size planets could fit in the Great Red Spot.

The Great Red Spot is thought to have winds reaching about 400 mph. That's almost two times faster than the strongest hurricane winds on Earth!

In the last 100 years, the Great Red Spot has shrunk. With so many other huge storms in the solar system, the Great Red Spot may not be the biggest for long.

AHHH,
THE GREAT RED SPOT.
NOT TO BE CONFUSED WITH
THE HORRIBLE BLUE SPOT,
THE ORDINARY ORANGE SPOT,
THE PUNGENT BROWN SPOT,
THE CURIOUS TEAL SPOT . . .

The Great Red Spot has been raging for at least 340 years!

THE GIGANTOR SUPERSTORM
THE GREAT RED SPOT (cont'd)

Jupiter has two high-speed jet streams that wrap around it, and the Great Red Spot sits comfortably between them, just south of the equator.

The NASA spacecraft Juno found that the Great Red Spot's roots go 50 to 100 times deeper than Earth's oceans!

NOW THAT IS A GREAT RED SPOT! . . . IS THAT WHAT I THINK IT IS?

I'M PRETTY SURE IT'S EITHER BARBECUE SAUCE . . . OR STRAWBERRY MILK . . . OR BOTH. YEAH, IT'S BOTH.

THE MOST BIGGEST-EST PLANET IN OUR SOLAR SYSTEM
JUPITER

Jupiter is the biggest planet in OUR SOLAR SYSTEM. More than 1,300 Earths could fit inside of Jupiter.

JUPITER

EARTH

JUPITER IS THE BIGGEST OF A GROUP OF PLANETS CALLED THE GAS GIANTS.

OTHER PLANETS IN THIS GROUP INCLUDE SATURN, URANUS, AND NEPTUNE. And Mr. DeMaio

Scientists think Jupiter has seventy-nine moons!

YEAH, BUT HOW MANY WATER PARKS DOES JUPITER HAVE?

NEARLY 273,000 MILES AROUND!

Jupiter's equator stretches nearly 273,000 miles around! It would take you over ten years to walk all the way around it!

WARNING!

THE STUFF YOU ARE ABOUT TO SEE IS

MEGA SUPER MACHO BIG!

SCIENTISTS ARE STILL LEARNING
ABOUT SOME OF THESE THINGS,
SO THERE AREN'T THAT MANY FACTS
ABOUT THEM,

BUT

WE DO HAVE AN IDEA OF HOW **BIG**
SOME OF THESE THINGS ARE.
PREPARE YOURSELF.

HA! HE SAID . . . BUT.

IT'S ABOUT TO GET HUGE!

HEY, GUYS! SOMEONE
JUST PUT THEIR HAND IN
MY POCKET. OH, WAIT, I
DON'T WEAR PANTS.

THE BIGGEST STUFF ~~BEYOND~~ THE S(E)AR SYSTEM

WHAT DID I DO TO DESERVE THIS!?!?!?!

THE BIGGEST STUFF ... BEYOND THE SOLAR SYSTEM!

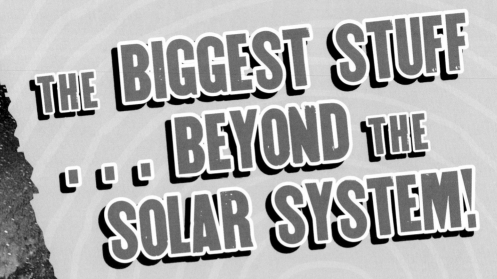

- ✦ Largest Exoplanet
- ✦ Biggest Star Known to Man
- ✦ Real Biggest Star Known to Man
- ✦ Largest Black Hole
- ✦ Most Gigantic-est Nebula Ever
- ✦ Biggest Galaxy!
- ✦ Gigantic Cosmic Structure
- ✦ Biggest Thing in the Known Universe

WOW . . . AND I THOUGHT MY EARS WERE BAD.

THE LARGEST EXOPLANET
HD 100546 b

HD 100546 b's mass is equal to 752 Jupiters.

x752

If Jupiter were the size of a Cheerio, HD 100546 b would be about the size of a baseball!

This exoplanet is roughly 320 light-years from Earth! Three hundred and twenty light-years is roughly equal to 1,881,160,119,418,755 miles.

HEY, DO YOU THINK THERE ARE ANY ALIENS ON THIS PLANET?

HD 100546 b is about seventy times farther from its star than the Earth is from the sun.

REALLY? THEY COULDN'T THINK OF ANYTHING COOLER LIKE MUSTAFAR OR TATOOINE?

OR JUPITER 2: WITH EXTRA JUPITERINESS

I'M NOT READY TO GO OUT LIKE THIS. I HAVE SO MANY QUESTIONS!

If you could travel by jet flying 600 mph to HD 100546 b, it would still take you 401 million years to get there!

THE BIGGEST STAR KNOWN TO MAN

TOM HANKS

He has been in more than fifty movies!

Tom Hanks has starred in such hits as *Toy Story, Toy Story 2, Toy Story 3, Toy Story 4, Toy Story 17: The Search for More Toy Stories,* and *Cloud Atlas.*

THIS GUY TALKED TO A BALL FOR TWO HOURS AND GOT NOMINATED FOR AN OSCAR, BUT WHEN I DO IT PEOPLE CALL THE COPS!

THE REAL BIGGEST STAR KNOWN TO MAN
UY SCUTI

UY Scuti is nearly 2,500 times bigger than HD 100546 b

HD 100546 b
× 2,500!

I'D CATCH YOU, BUT I HAVE NO ARMS.

There are many different types of stars. UY Scuti is one of the biggest types, called a red supergiant. Red supergiants are some of the biggest stars in the universe!

LET HIM FALL! IT'S NOT LIKE THERE'S A GIANT FIERY DEATH BALL BEHIND HIM OR ANYTHING.

THE REAL BIGGEST STAR KNOWN TO MAN
UY SCUTI (cont'd)

UY Scuti's radius is 1,700 times bigger than our sun. Roughly four billion suns could fit inside of it!

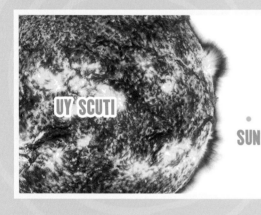

UY SCUTI

SUN

TAKE THAT, YOU FOUL BEAST!

UY Scuti can be found in the Scutum Constellation. Scutum is Latin for shield.

UY Scuti is so big that if you swapped it out with our sun, it would stretch all the way to the orbit of Saturn. That means it could fit five planets, over eighty moons, and the asteroid belt all jam-packed into ONE STAR!

EARTH

SUN

THE LARGEST BLACK HOLE
(so far)
TON 618

It's believed to be over 240 billion miles wide! That's equal to nearly one million trips around the equator on Earth!

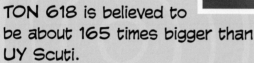

x 1,000,000

TON 618 is believed to be about 165 times bigger than UY Scuti.

x165

THE EVENT HORIZON IS THE PART OF THE BLACK HOLE WHERE LIGHT CANNOT ESCAPE. WHEN AN OBJECT CROSSES THE EVENT HORIZON, IT IS STRETCHED INTO LONG THIN SHAPES, LIKE PASTA. THIS PROCESS IS CALLED SPAGHETTIFICATION!

TON 618 is something called a quasar. Inside of the quasar is something called an ultramassive black hole. Scientists believe that the black hole at the center of this quasar may be the biggest they've ever found!

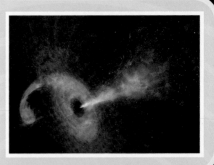

THIS MAY NOT BE A BAD LOOK FOR ME.

SPAGHETTI?!? BUT I HAVE A SLIGHT GLUTEN INTOLERANCE!

It could swallow our entire solar system and ask for seconds. In fact, if you were to put the supermassive black hole at the center of TON 618 in the center of our solar system, it would stretch far beyond the reaches of Pluto!

THE MOST GIGANTIC-EST NEBULA EVER
TARANTULA NEBULA

It is believed to be about four quadrillion miles wide! That's nearly 2.6 million times bigger than UY Scuti, the biggest star known to man, and about 16,000 times bigger than TON 618!

UY SCUTI

✖ NEARLY 2.6 MILLION

TON 618

✖ ABOUT 16,000

The Tarantula Nebula got its name from its bright patches that look like spider legs. It also has another name, 30 Doradus.

The Tarantula Nebula is about 940 quadrillion miles from Earth!

HOW DID WE ALL SURVIVE THE BLACK HOLE ON THE LAST PAGE?

WE DIDN'T. WE'RE THEIR STUNT DOUBLES.

THE BIGGEST GALAXY!

IC 1101

The IC 1101 galaxy is believed to be about 6,000 times bigger than the Tarantula Nebula, 95 million times bigger than TON 618, and over 15 billion times bigger than UY Scuti!

WHOA! IC 1101!!!

TARANTULA NEBULA

✖ ABOUT 6,000

TON 618

✖ ABOUT 95 MILLION

UY SCUTI

✖ ABOUT 15 BILLION

There are many different types of galaxies, but IC 1101 is a supergiant elliptical galaxy.

IC 1101 has the mass of about 100 trillion stars!

DOESN'T LOOK SO ICY TO ME. SHOULD BE CALLED "SPINNY SPARKLY 1101."

WHAT? I DON'T SEE ANY 1101S ANYWHERE.

CAN WE PULL OVER? I HAVE TO GO NUMBER THREE . . .

If you *could* travel in a Lamborghini at its top speed on a bridge from Earth to IC 1101, it would take you about 3,170,252,800,137,842 years!

THE GIGANTIC COSMIC STRUCTURE
SLOAN GREAT WALL

You thought IC 1101 was big? Well, the Sloan Great Wall is believed to be 350 times bigger and over 2 Million times bigger than the Tarantula Nebula!

IF IT IS A SPACE GOAT, WE SHOULD PROBABLY TELL THE READER ABOUT IT.

The Sloan Great Wall Thingy is a Space Goat

ALREADY ON IT . . .

The Sloan Great Wall is a cosmic structure formed by a giant wall of galaxies, called a galaxy filament.

THE BIGGEST THING IN THE KNOWN UNIVERSE
HERCULES-CORONA BOREALIS GREAT WALL

The Hercules-Corona Borealis Great Wall is a galactic filament, an enormous group of galaxies bound together by gravity.

Some scientists believe that the Great Wall contains over four billion galaxies!

It is believed to be measured at 10 million light-years across. For comparison, the Milky Way galaxy is only about 100 thousand light-years across.

✱ 4 BILLION

SLOAN GREAT WALL

✱ ABOUT 8

IC 1101

✱ ABOUT 3,000

TARANTULA NEBULA

✱ ABOUT 16 MILLION

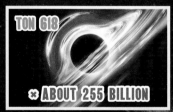

TON 618

✱ ABOUT 255 BILLION

UY SCUTI

✱ ABOUT 42 TRILLION

It is about 8 times bigger than the Sloan Great Wall, nearly 3,000 times bigger than IC 1101, about 16 million times bigger than the Tarantula Nebula, roughly 255 billion times bigger than TON 618, and nearly 42 trillion times bigger than UY Scuti!

This massive structure defies its own existence. Experts aren't even sure how something like this came to be.

GROSSET & DUNLAP
An imprint of Penguin Random House LLC, New York

First published in the United States of America by Grosset & Dunlap,
an imprint of Penguin Random House LLC, New York, 2022

Visit us online at penguinrandomhouse.com.

Library of Congress Cataloging-in-Publication Data is available.

Manufactured in Canada

ISBN 9780593224809   10 9 8 7 6 5 4 3 2 1 TC

The publisher does not have any control over and does not assume any
responsibility for author or third-party websites or their content.